IMAGES
of America

AROUND ROXBURY

IMAGES
of America

AROUND ROXBURY

Anthony Liberatore and
Lynette Hinkley Liberatore

ARCADIA
PUBLISHING

Published by Arcadia Publishing
Charleston, South Carolina

Library of Congress Control Number: 2012952625

For all general information, please contact Arcadia Publishing:
Telephone 843-853-2070
Fax 843-853-0044
E-mail sales@arcadiapublishing.com
For customer service and orders:
Toll-Free 1-888-313-2665

Visit us on the Internet at www.arcadiapublishing.com

Dedicated to the memory of Ronnie Ballard and Irma Mae Griffin

CONTENTS

ACKNOWLEDGMENTS

Many people were instrumental in assembling and writing this book. We sincerely appreciate the lending of photographs and the trust we were granted while scanning and documenting each one. The personal collections of Lynda Stratton, Kathy Roberts, and Larry Cartwright were fascinating treasure troves to peruse and choose from. Danny Underwood contributed photographs taken by his mother, Lena Underwood, and was always ready to offer his memories and information about local history. The collections of the Delaware County Historical Society (DCHS), the Town of Roxbury (TOR), the Jay Gould Memorial Reformed Church, and the Roxbury Library Association (RLA) were also great resources of photographs.

Asking questions of our knowledgeable history mentors was probably the most rewarding part of creating this book. We learned more with nearly every caption written. Instrumental in that task were Grand Gorge residents Willard Palmer, Mike Ciaravino, and Dorothy and Preston Van Dusen. Olive Van Aken, Esther Snyder, and Doris Kelly patiently answered questions and offered up family photographs as well. Possibly the most valuable research assistance came from Irma Mae Griffin's book *The History of the Town of Roxbury*. The archives of the *Catskill Mountain News* provided us an informative way to dig a little deeper into the past as well.

We also want to thank our Arcadia Publishing acquisitions editor, Remy Thurston, for all of his assistance with this project.

Last, but far from least, the friendship and education provided by the late Ronnie Ballard was a true inspiration and spurs us on to keep learning about the history around Roxbury.

INTRODUCTION

The town of Roxbury had its beginnings in Moresville. The More family came to the area in the late 1700s, and the roots of what would become Grand Gorge were established. John More built the first log cabin in Grand Gorge and had a tavern at the site of the current village square. It proved to be an excellent location, becoming an important stop on the route from the Hudson River to New York City.

Members of the More family and additional settlers spread south, and by 1790, settlements were popping up in Roxbury. The Vega Valley followed, with the Keator family staking their claim in 1794. Hunting and trapping sustained the early settlers, followed by farming. Farming started as a necessity, providing food for each individual family. Early farmers raised animals for meat, eggs, and dairy and produced their own supply of maple sugar and honey from their own bees. Rye was grown for bread, and flax was produced to be spun into linen for clothing.

As roads and transportation improved, local farmers were able to buy more supplies for their daily needs and could pursue commercial farming. Dairy farming became an important industry in the area. The uneven land, rich with natural springs, was found to be ideal for raising dairy cows and less so for growing commercial crops. The butter industry started in the late 1700s, when David Smith first packed and sold his butter. Other farmers followed his lead, and soon, Roxbury was well known for its wonderful butter, and it became a leading industry. With the arrival of the railroad, shipping milk became a possibility as well. The first shipment of milk left Roxbury in 1878. Creameries were built to process the milk and prepare it for shipping. The milk train was a great source of income for the railroad for many years.

As the train took dairy products out of the area, it also brought visitors to the area. In the 1870s, many city dwellers discovered the fresh, cool air and the scenic beauty of the Roxbury area. Boardinghouses and inns were built to house the visitors. Farmers opened their doors and rented out their spare rooms for additional income. Women and children spent their summers in the mountains, and husbands arrived on trains for the weekends. The 1960s brought skiers to the area, and the need for winter lodging followed. In more recent years, many visitors to the area have been so reluctant to leave that they have purchased second homes, and some of them have even made the transition to full-time residents.

The Gould and Shepard family had a beneficial influence on the town, leaving many notable landmarks and assisting the town in hard financial times. Kirkside Park, the Jay Gould Memorial Reformed Church, the Roxbury Arts Group, the Roxbury Library, and Shephard Hills Golf Course have all benefitted directly or indirectly from the generosity of the Gould family. Many local residents worked for the Shepards during the Depression and beyond. Writer and naturalist John Burroughs loved Roxbury, and through his writings, he taught millions of people to enjoy the nature he first discovered on a farm near West Settlement.

The hamlets of Grand Gorge and Roxbury boasted a wide array of stores from the 1800s to the mid-1900s. Townspeople could find almost all they needed from local merchants. Dry goods stores, butcher shops, pharmacies, wagon shops, and car dealerships were available just a short wagon ride—and later, car ride—away. Entertainment was available locally as well. Concerts, movies, sports, and clubs kept people busy after the work was done.

Today the town of Roxbury enjoys a variety of residents, both full-time and part-time. Some residents can trace their local family tree back to the 1800s, and some have only recently discovered the area's rural charms and the lure of the mountains. Two things they have in common are the desire to enjoy all that Roxbury has to offer and the need to protect and maintain this unique and beautiful place.

One

Living and Working in Grand Gorge

This north-facing view of Grand Gorge shows a lightly populated village. The stately steeple of the Methodist church can be seen at the northern edge of town. The many mountains surrounding the village inspired the name Grand Gorge. (Courtesy of TOR, Ronnie Ballard collection.)

In 1897, T.W. Decker and Sons built and operated this creamery just south of Grand Gorge, near the Ulster & Delaware Railroad tracks. After a few years, the creamery changed hands and was called Sheffield Farms–Slawson–Decker Company. Raymond F. Cronk rebuilt the creamery in 1917, and it eventually closed in 1963. The site is now the home of Becker's Tire Service. (Courtesy of Preston Van Dusen.)

The Ulster & Delaware Railroad arrived at Grand Gorge, milepost 65, on August 8, 1872. Herman Krum was the station agent for about seven years until it closed in 1954. The Grand Gorge station was torn down around 1960. (Courtesy of Mark Proper.)

Dr. Morton J. Vogt poses with his car in this undated photograph. Dr. Vogt practiced in Grand Gorge from 1911 to 1947. He once lived on Vogt Lane (now Becker Lane), but he died in his Ferris Hill home in 1948. (Courtesy of RLA.)

Beginning in the early 1800s, this location was home to a grocery store. The last grocer was Samuel J. Draffen, who operated the store until the 1930s. George and Anna Ploutz moved from their Roxbury home to operate a bar and restaurant in the former store, on Route 30 just south of Grand Gorge. Anna continued to run the business after George's death in 1956. After her retirement, their daughter Elsie Proper ran the restaurant. (Courtesy of Mark Proper.)

The Independent Order of Odd Fellows was organized in the area in 1895. George Donohue was the first noble grand. The order disbanded in 1934. Sidney Kelly and Walter Hunt used the building as a movie house for a few years around 1910. It was the first location within the Town of Roxbury to show movies. The building was located on Route 30 just north of the current Grand Gorge firehouse. It was torn down in 1946. (Courtesy of Preston Van Dusen.)

Just to the right of the Odd Fellows hall was the garage of Lester Joslyn. He originally ran a blacksmith shop but started the garage business when cars started to become more popular than horses. Joslyn is seen here in 1923. (Courtesy of Grand Gorge Fire Department.)

Jordan's Ice Cream was a popular establishment in Grand Gorge where one could get lunch, sodas, and ice cream and bowl a few games. It later turned into the Village Inn, and after the building burned, the lot became home to the new Grand Gorge firehouse. (Courtesy of Daniel Underwood.)

The Truck Stop Diner, on Route 23 north of Grand Gorge, grew from a gas station into a diner that also offered curb and roadside service, tourist homes, cottages, a gas station, and a trailer park. Owners Henry and Josephine Widemann operated the business until 1964. Walter and Herminia Behrens purchased the diner from them and operated it until 1970. The building was painted pink for a time, and the business was nicknamed the Pink Pig. (Courtesy of Lynda Stratton.)

The Grand Gorge Diner was delivered to its new home on January 29, 1942. An addition for the kitchen and bathrooms was added to the diner after it was positioned on the site. The new diner could seat 36 people. (Courtesy of Olive Van Aken.)

Built on the site of the Streeter house, the Grand Gorge Diner, seen in the background of this parade, was built by Roy and Elizabeth Streeter in 1942. The diner was well known for its great food and excellent service. The Streeters' children and their spouses continued running the diner after their parents' deaths in 1966 and 1967. The diner was sold in 1971 to Anthony Colucci and was destroyed by fire in 1988. (Courtesy of RLA.)

Arriving from Lincolnshire, England, around 1805, the Joseph H. Dent family settled on Ferris Hill in Grand Gorge. Charles J. Dent was the third generation to run the farm. John Thorington, a cousin of Charles's, was the next owner and operated the farm with his sons Stanley and David. The farmhouse is seen above in 1961. (Courtesy of Stanley Thorington.)

Charles Dent poses in front of his barns at his farm on Dent Road in Grand Gorge in October 1951. (Courtesy of Stanley Thorington.)

John Thorington married his neighbor Catherine Murray, and members of both families gathered for this family photograph on the Dent farm. From left to right are (first row) Barbara Thorington, Ann Thorington, and Stanley Thorington; (second row) unidentified, Catherine Murray Thorington, ? Murray, and Charles Dent; (third row) John Thorington, Gertrude Murray, and Manley Murray. (Courtesy of Stanley Thorington.)

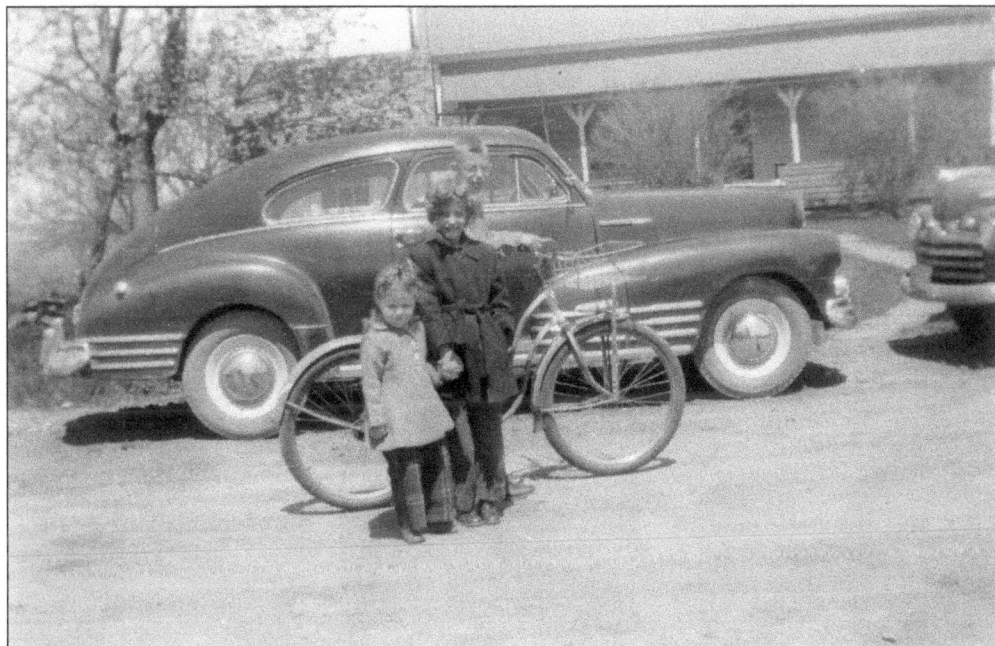

Seen here taking a break from playing outdoors with a bicycle are, from left to right, siblings Barbara, Ann, and Stanley Thorington. The photograph was taken in 1951, when the Thorington children were visiting the farm of their grandfather Manley Murray. (Courtesy of Stanley Thorington.)

Elwood Clark owned a restaurant and inn in Gilboa, New York, which became a victim of eminent domain when the Gilboa dam project was built. Clark's father-in-law, Omar Yanson, built a new hotel and restaurant for Clark and his wife, Edna, in Grand Gorge. Before the hotel was completed, however, Prohibition kicked in. The Clarks ran a fruit and vegetable stand in the front of the building, but the back of the building was a speakeasy. Elwood reportedly picked up the illegal beverages in Cairo for his own and other local businesses, while Edna brewed beer upstairs. Their grandson Vern Bailey recounted a story of his grandmother speaking with local policemen in the vegetable stand while watching beer drip down through the ceiling. (Courtesy of DCHS, Bob Wyer collection.)

This interior shot of the Grand Gorge Hotel was taken after Prohibition ended in 1933, as the fully loaded bar is in clear view. Later owners of the hotel included Nat and Lil Bernstein, and, by 1955, Gerard and Victoria O'Gormley. (Courtesy of DCHS, Bob Wyer collection.)

The Hardenburg house was built in the early 1800s at the eastern edge of Grand Gorge, on Route 23. Isaac Hardenburg built the stone mansion with the finest materials and labor. Hardenburg had a store in the basement of the house and a sawmill and a gristmill nearby. The post office of Hardenburg Mills was established in the house on October 2, 1815. The wooden porches were added in the early 1900s and have since been removed. The house remained in the Hardenburg family until the 1930s. (Courtesy of the author.)

Schuyler Colfax Pindar had a livestock and livery stable on this site prior to 1915. When his son Frank Simonson Pindar joined the business in 1915, he started a garage but also continued the livestock business for a few more years. As the need for horses and carriages declined, however, that part of the business was dropped. Frank Simonson Pindar's son and grandsons all worked at the family business until it closed in 1991. (Courtesy of TOR, Ronnie Ballard collection.)

Possibly occupying the same site as the first store in Moresville—the 1822 business of Jonas Laraway More—this store was first owned by George A. Dent in the 1850s. After taking part in the California Gold Rush, Charles Harley purchased, rebuilt, and enlarged the store in 1856. Harley offered feed, coal, and dry goods. In 1941, the general store (center section) burned, and it was rebuilt as the Oneida store. Upon her death in 1943, Lulu More Harley left the coal and feed store (right section) to her longtime manager, Wilbur Joslyn. (Courtesy of Grand Gorge Fire Department.)

The Joslyn feed store was next door to the original Harley store. Here, the Earl B. Dudley American Legion Post proudly marches by the store in a Memorial Day parade. Unable to work due to illness, Wilbur Joslyn sold the building in 1963 to Elmer Alberti, who tore it down for the lumber. (Courtesy of the author.)

Draffen's store was originally a butcher shop built in the 1880s by Christopher Deyo. William H. Draffen purchased the store in 1898, first selling dry goods there. In 1930, Draffen sold the business to his son Ralph, who ran the shoe store until his death in 1956. His widow, Helen, continued running the store into the 1970s. (Courtesy of Preston Van Dusen.)

This view of Grand Gorge's business center shows a narrow, dirt version of Route 23 heading west. The large building on the right was home to two businesses. The open door seen here was the entrance to the H.D. Booth grocery and feed. The Victory Market occupied the western portion of the building. (Courtesy of RLA.)

The Grand Gorge Hose Company was formed in 1897, the same year George Decker donated a hand-drawn hose cart. This brick fire station was built in 1936 on Route 23. The upper floor was for the use of fire department members. The hose company moved to a new building on Route 30 in 2003, adding square footage for equipment and a large, comfortable space for community gatherings. (Courtesy of Grand Gorge Fire Department.)

In 1955, the Grand Gorge Hose Company purchased this American LaFrance pumper. Seen here are, from left to right, Joe Magro, Frank Kolts, Bob Murray, and an unidentified man. The location of this burning building is unknown. (Courtesy of Grand Gorge Fire Department.)

The Grand Gorge National Bank was organized in 1905. The first officers were Samuel Harley, president; Arthur F. Bouton, vice president; and Orrin Day Wood, cashier. In 1957, the bank became a branch of the National Bank and Trust Company of Norwich. The small wooden building on the right was the first home of the bank. (Courtesy of Preston Van Dusen.)

The grounds of the Devasago Inn, seen here, were in the northeast corner of the Town of Roxbury, near Prattsville. The property was the summer home of the Smedberg family from 1827 to 1898. Starr D. and Lottie Mase operated the property as an inn from 1898 to the 1920s. In 1915, a dam and power plant were constructed above the Devasago Falls to provide water and power for the inn. Here, a warm summer day draws a group of swimmers to Devasago Falls after the closing of the inn. (Courtesy of TOR.)

Samuel Harley was the great-grandson of Thomas Harley, a pioneer of the Ferris Hill area of Grand Gorge. Samuel was a merchant in Grand Gorge after inheriting a store from his father in 1890. A leading citizen in Grand Gorge, he was also postmaster and the founder of Grand Gorge Bank. His beautiful home, just east of the village square on Route 23, is seen here. (Courtesy of TOR, Ronnie Ballard collection.)

Two

THE VEGA AND
DENVER VALLEY

Peleg and Martha Ballard settled in the north end of the Batavia-Kill Valley (now Vega) in 1794. They were the first settlers in that part of the valley. The farm has passed from father to son ever since, and the current residents are the eighth generation of Ballards to live there. The farmhouse is seen here in 1941, when it was occupied by John and Nellie Bly Ballard. (Courtesy of James Ballard.)

This was once the farm of Jonathon and Virtue Ballard. Their daughter Ora was born in 1899 and grew up to marry Floyd Sherwood. Floyd and Ora's son Harvey and his wife, Flora, then owned and worked the farm until passing it on to their son and his wife, Gary and Kathy Thompson Sherwood. Gary and Kathy eventually sold the family farm and moved their farming business to western New York. (Courtesy of Betty Sherwood.)

The Sherwood farmhouse is seen here. This farm sits at the northeastern edge of the Vega Valley. The farm's first owner, Jonathan Ballard, was born in 1863 and was buried in the Vega cemetery when he died in 1939. (Courtesy of Betty Sherwood.)

A full wagonload of milk cans is ready for transport in this early-1900s photograph. Holding the reins is Jonathan Ballard, with his daughter Ora next to him. (Courtesy of Betty Sherwood.)

Leo Finch was a farmer in Denver and also sold Silver King tractors. Below, Leo and his new bride, Carrie Angle Finch, prepare to leave on their honeymoon. They were married on November 4, 1922. (Courtesy of Larry Cartwright.)

Floyd Sherwood is seen here with a fairly unusual pet for a farmer, a deer. Floyd was a descendant of Moses Sherwood, a sharpshooter in the War of 1812. Floyd and his three sons, Harvey, Francis, and Julian, each farmed in the Vega Valley. (Courtesy of Julian Sherwood.)

Nellie Bly Shultis Ballard was named by her father after the world-traveling journalist Nellie Bly, who was in the news around the time of her birth. She was called the local "Grandma Moses" because of her primitive paintings of historical buildings and landscapes. One of her paintings is behind her in this photograph. She died in 1971. (Courtesy of James Ballard.)

Shotguns in hand, these men are ready for a day of hunting. They are, from left to right, Low Bennet, Eli Finch, Eli Jenkins, and two unidentified men. Eli Finch was Eber Cartwright's father-in-law. (Courtesy of Larry Cartwright.)

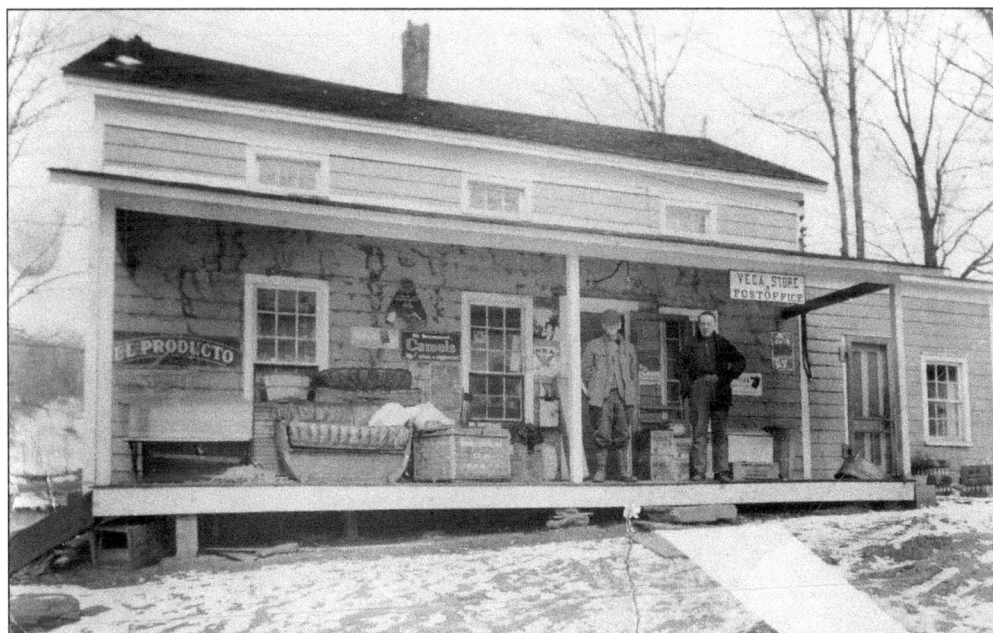

The Vega post office was established on December 20, 1895. William B. Kelly, the postmaster, was given the task of naming the post office. He submitted a few options, and the post office department chose Vega. Kelly also kept a store, which was sold along with the post office to Leland Craft in 1927. In this 1932 photograph of the Vega store and post office, Oscar Germonds is on the left and Leland Craft is on the right. (Courtesy of Lynda Stratton.)

Elizabeth Morse was one of the first people to take in boarders, at her home in the Denver-Vega area. After retiring, her son Henry W. Morse and his wife, Beulah Roberts Morse, continued to take in boarders at the Morse farm. Henry was also a businessman in Roxbury, renting and operating a garage behind Dixon Manor. He later moved his business across the street and formed a partnership with LaMoure Stewart. Together, they ran the Cities service station. (Courtesy of Kathryn Roberts.)

This view of the Henry W. Morse farm was taken from the back side of the farm. Scudder Hill Road runs along the front of the house. The many cleared fields necessary for farming and the lack of additional homes presents a very different view than today. The Morse family boardinghouse business ceased when the home was sold in 1960. (Courtesy of Lynda Stratton.)

The Roberts family came to Delaware County in 1815. The son or grandson of that first family moved to Batavia-Kill some time after that, to the area now known as Vega. This farm was owned by Wells Roberts and remained in the Roberts family for five generations. Today, a member of that fifth generation, Kevin Roberts, owns some of the family land and continues the farming tradition. (Courtesy of Kathryn Roberts.)

This Vega farm and boardinghouse was operated by Joseph Parker Morse and his wife, Bertha. This 1912 photograph shows city boarders gathered on the lawn and porches. In the 1960s, the farm was sold and the land was subdivided for a development called Roxbury Run. The farmhouse was converted into a clubhouse and then a restaurant. The Roxbury Run Restaurant was purchased by Walter and Jacqueline Keller in 1971 and has since closed. (Courtesy of Cathy Cammer.)

The Cartwright family descended from Bailey and Asenath Cartwright, a pioneer family in the Vega Valley. Their son Eber married Polly Ganoug. In 1898, Eber's farm was home to one of the first cooperative creameries in the area, which closed in 1918. Eber's grandson Charles V. Cartwright is seen here with a team of horses raking his freshly cut hay. (Courtesy of Larry Cartwright.)

Dora Cartwright and a dapper but unidentified companion pose for a photograph on the hood of an automobile at the farm in 1931. (Courtesy of Larry Cartwright.)

Charles V. Cartwright's son, Eber, named for his great-grandfather, worked the family farm in the 1940s. This June 1941 photograph shows his new barn being built, with the framing just starting to take shape. Sanford Hinkley of Roxbury was the builder of the barn. (Courtesy of Larry Cartwright.)

Much progress can be seen in this shot of Eber Cartwright's new barn, with the second story well underway and the roof starting to take shape. The Cartwright farm was called Ponderosa. (Courtesy of Larry Cartwright.)

Eber Cartwright is seen above on his tractor during hay season in the summer of 1952. The farm implement behind his tractor is a bailer. (Courtesy of Larry Cartwright.)

With the barn now completed, the first of the hay is loaded in. Horses were still being used on this family farm in 1941, and the hay is un-baled and loaded into the barn using a hay grapple. (Courtesy of Larry Cartwright.)

A neatly stacked truckload of hay is headed to the Cartwright family barn in 1952. The coal delivery truck was owned by Dick Finch, who also worked with the Cartwright family during hay season. (Courtesy of Larry Cartwright.)

A descendant of the Cartwright family in Batavia-Kill, Maj. George Cartwright was born in 1862, the son of Dr. Silas Cartwright. After graduating from West Point in 1885, he began his military career. While serving in Matanzas, Cuba, he was quartermaster and chief of street cleaning. He improved street conditions and reduced the death rate from yellow fever. Unfortunately, he contracted yellow fever himself, and died on September 23, 1900. This photograph shows his burial at the Roxbury Methodist cemetery. (Courtesy of TOR, Ronnie Ballard collection.)

The Denver Post Office, seen here facing towards the camera, was established on March 12, 1892. Henrietta Jenkins chose that name for the post office because she thought the hilly terrain might be similar to that of Denver, Colorado. The building also housed a store. On the hill behind the post office is the Eli Finch farm. (Courtesy of Lynda Stratton.)

The Roxbury Ski Center was on the upper end of Vega Valley on Batavia-Kill Mountain. It opened in 1957. Snowy winters ensured success for the first few seasons. The ski area changed ownership and names several times. It was known as Big Bear and later as Noname Ski Area. This photograph shows the modern lodge in the background, with its double bank of windows designed to take advantage of sunny days. The ski area closed in the 1970s after several seasons of poor snowfall. (Courtesy of the author.)

Three

IN AND AROUND THE
HAMLET OF ROXBURY

43—Birdseye View, Roxbury, N. Y.

This bird's-eye view of Roxbury provides a picturesque image of the village. The many cleared fields were the result of a lot of backbreaking work by local farmers. On the far right is the tower of the Jay Gould Memorial Reformed Church, on the north end of the village. (Courtesy of the author.)

The More family monument is located in the Roxbury cemetery. It was erected and dedicated in September 1890, during the first More family reunion. The monument is carved with the names of Betty and John More and each of their eight children. This photograph was taken at the 1900 reunion. The reunions are still held every five years, specifically in years ending in zero or five. (Courtesy of TOR, Ronnie Ballard collection.)

The stately Frisbee house, on the north end of Main Street, was built in 1829 by John Frisbee. The house was sold out of the family but repurchased in 1908 by John Frisbee's namesake grandson, John Frisbee Keator, who moved the house back from the street and enlarged it, adding a right wing and a third floor with dormers and sleeping porches. John Keator's wife, Anna Sweatman Keator, was a cousin to Helen Gould. (Courtesy of the author.)

In early times, Hubbell Corners was known as North Roxbury. The first Hubbell in the area was Patrick F. Hubbell, a highly skilled workman. This charming view, looking to the east from Route 30, shows many fine open fields for farming. Today, the same view shows the fields inhabited by some houses and many more trees. (Courtesy of the author.)

The area surrounding Hardscrabble Road and Burroughs Memorial Road was once known as Pleasant Valley. John Persons moved to the area around 1800, building a temporary sawmill to produce the wood needed to construct a gristmill. Later, his grandson John Person More ran the gristmill and rebuilt the sawmill. George Robinson purchased the two mills and operated them until a flood washed out the dam for the gristmill in 1889. This photograph was taken when the home was owned by Addison and Alice More in the early 1900s. (Courtesy of RLA.)

The worst train wreck of the Ulster & Delaware Railroad occurred on May 26, 1922. As a work train and crew were backing up from Roxbury to Grand Gorge, they were struck by a southbound freight train. The work train had a crane attacked to the caboose, and the six men in the caboose were killed. The deceased included Fred Chase and Fred Loudon of Grand Gorge and Fred Borst of Roxbury. Alonzo Hait and Jacob Steinhelder, also Grand Gorge residents, were on the back platform and managed to jump to safety. (Courtesy of Doris Kelly.)

The accident was blamed on a misunderstanding of train orders. The work train was picking up waste metal, cleaning sluices, and unloading steel rails. The freight train was loaded with coal and headed to Arkville. The work train was expected to go on a siding while the freight train passed, but the freight train came earlier than expected. (Courtesy of Doris Kelly.)

Despite the massive amount of wreckage on the tracks, crews were able to push the locomotive aside and clear a path through the debris so that trains could run on the tracks the very next day. (Courtesy of Doris Kelly.)

The accident occurred in the area now known as the Long Woods. The cars in this photograph are parked on Route 30. This unfortunate event brought a number of curious onlookers out to get a first-hand look at the tragedy. (Courtesy of Doris Kelly.)

This mountain is called White Man Mountain because a flat-faced rock midway up the mountain was painted with the figure of a man by 10-year-old Marcy Powell in 1860. Powell took a pail of whitewash with him up the mountain and painted the rock as his father planted potatoes. His father was attempting to plant potatoes so high up that the Colorado potato beetle could not find them. The mountain has been a favorite hike of adults and children for generations. (Courtesy of the author.)

The Van Aken children of Montgomery Hollow in Roxbury enjoy some winter sledding fun around 1940. Posing with their sleds are, from left to right, (first row) Robert, Alvin, Doris, and Eleanor Van Aken; (second row) Otis and Millard Van Aken. (Courtesy of Doris Kelly.)

The Ulster & Delaware Railroad reached Roxbury on December 28, 1871. The line originally stopped south of the village, in Strattons Falls, but, by 1872, it had been extended to Roxbury and on to Stamford. The location of the station moved the business section from upper Main Street to Bridge Street and the current village square. Passenger service ended in Roxbury in 1954, and freight trains ceased running in 1976. (Courtesy of TOR, Ronnie Ballard collection.)

The viaduct that crossed Route 30 in Hubbell Corners was constructed in 1914, when several trains a day traveled the Ulster & Delaware tracks. As trains ran less frequently between Kingston and Stamford, the viaduct was no longer a necessity by the 1970s. Trains ceased running altogether on this line in 1976. This 1979 photograph shows the train tracks already removed in preparation for the elimination of the viaduct and the rerouting of Route 30. (Courtesy of Marion Gile.)

Edward Burhans built and owned this beautiful Main Street home in the 1880s. Dr. Charles Henry Snow and his wife, Alice Northrup Snow, purchased the house in 1897 as a summer home. The Snows were married on May 17, 1897, at a ceremony in the newly completed Jay Gould Memorial Reformed Church. Alice was a cousin of Helen Gould Shepard and wrote a biography of her cousin called *The Story of Helen Gould*. Dr. Snow was the dean of the College of Engineering at New York University for 30 years. After his retirement in 1930, they spent quite a bit of time at their Roxbury home. (Courtesy of Daniel Underwood.)

Edward Burhans also built this home in 1880. It was owned by local attorney Frank Andrus. After his death in 1913, the home was purchased by Dr. Gilbert J. Palen and his wife, Anna. In 1959, after their parents' deaths, Dr. Gilbert M. Palen and John Burr Gould Palen gave the house to the Jay Gould Memorial Reformed Church. For 14 years, the church used the house for Sunday school, women's meetings, social events, and wedding receptions. The church sold the house in the 1970s, and it was once again a private home. (Courtesy of Daniel Underwood.)

These children had the right idea for traveling on Roxbury's appropriately named Lake Street, which often flooded until drainage improvements were made in 1972. A boat seems to have been the best choice in this 1941 photograph, with Danny Underwood supplying the rowing power in the far back. The street was called Frog Alley in earlier days because of the spring peepers that chirped in the area, announcing the arrival of spring. (Courtesy of Daniel Underwood.)

This Main Street view shows Reed's Hotel on the far left and Dr. Julian A. Gaul's home next to it. Dr. Gaul moved to the area from Milton-on-Hudson and married Maud Van Dyke, a local Roxbury girl. They purchased the home in 1917 and lived there until their deaths. She died in December 1957, and he died a month later. (Courtesy of Lynda Stratton.)

The first fire department in Roxbury, named the B.B. Bouton Hose Company, was organized on September 2, 1890. A hose cart was purchased in January 1891. A second fire company, the Hook and Ladder Company, was organized on November 2, 1892, after Helen M. Gould gifted the community with a hook and ladder truck and a Babcock fire extinguisher. The two groups combined to form the Roxbury Fire Department in 1929. This photograph shows a Sanford truck purchased in April 1929 (left) and a Chevrolet truck purchased in February 1937 (right). The firehouse was on Main Street in the building that now houses the Roxbury Town Hall. (Courtesy of the Roxbury Fire Department.)

The Fanning store building was torn down to make way for a new firehouse, as the old one needed to be replaced by 1966. The new, modern, fireproof building provided space for a growing collection of equipment, as well as meeting and community space. The dedication of the new building was held on April 15, 1967. (Courtesy of the Roxbury Fire Department.)

The first elected fire chief, Elton LaRue, served from 1948 to 1975. LaRue, who appears to be dressed for a parade, poses here in front of Roxbury Central School with fire trucks and an antique hose cart. (Courtesy of the Roxbury Fire Department.)

The Roxbury Concert Band poses for a photograph on the chapel steps of the Jay Gould Memorial Reformed Church. The band provided entertainment at various events around town, including the 1910 More reunion at a luncheon hosted by Helen M. Gould. (Courtesy of TOR, Ronnie Ballard collection.)

The first group of Masons in Roxbury was established in 1825 and was active for five years. The charter was revoked in 1835. The next group was formed in 1865. After meeting in various locations for years, the new, permanent home for the Masons was built in 1884 on the site of W.H. Plough's wagon shop. The Masons were active for 107 years. The Masonic hall is now home to the local WIOX radio station. (Courtesy of RLA.)

YOURSELF AND LADIES ARE CORDIALLY INVITED TO ATTEND THE

. . . . . ST. PATRICK'S DANCE . . . . .

TO BE HELD AT

MASONIC HALL, ROXBURY, N. Y.,

FRIDAY EVENING, MARCH 15, 1912.

MUSIC FURNISHED BY MEAD'S FOUR PIECE ORCHESTRA

DANCING AT 8:30.   BILL 75 CENTS.

INVITE ALL YOUR FRIENDS.

The Masonic hall hosted many groups and events, including this St. Patrick's Day dance in 1912. (Courtesy of TOR, Ronnie Ballard collection.)

In 1852, Hamilton Burhans traded this home, which he built in 1847, along with his Main Street tin shop, for the Gould homestead and farm in West Settlement. In 1895, Helen Gould bought the building and founded Roxbury's first public library in the front part of the building. In 1939, the library was moved to the newly completed central school. In 1976, a renovated Main Street building became the new home of the public library. (Courtesy of RLA.)

The local chapter of the Young Men's Christian Association (YMCA) was organized in 1904. The building, a gift from Helen Gould Shepard in 1911, is seen here at its dedication. The building was used as a gymnasium by the Roxbury School and was used by the first and second grades before the new school was built. The Delaware Valley Grange purchased the building in 1942. The building is now part of the Roxbury Arts Group and is home to Hilt Kelly Hall and the Walt Meade Gallery. (Courtesy of TOR, Ronnie Ballard collection.)

The Independent Order of Odd Fellows was organized in Roxbury in 1891. One form of entertainment for the group was performing costumed skits. The woman on the far left here is Leona Dugan, and Andy Underwood is the man on the right in a top hat. Continuing to the right from him are Josephine Caswell, Dewitt Preston, and Carry Rutshouser. The woman sitting in the front row is Ethel Underwood, and the two young girls are Belva (left) and Jean Tyler. (Courtesy of Daniel Underwood.)

These ladies take a summer stroll through a field overlooking New Kingston Mountain Road. In the background is a stone house built in 1828 by Walter Stratton. In this small house, Stratton and his wife, Esther, raised eight children. After having several owners, the house was purchased by John Corbin. Later, Corbin's daughter Lena inherited the house. It is now owned by the Manhattan Country School. (Courtesy of the author.)

Built by Christian Enderlin in the late 1800s, this was the home of Frank Enderlin, a local businessman who purchased a hardware store from Alexander Burhans in 1895. (Courtesy of the author.)

This building served as the Roxbury Post Office from 1905 until 1955, when the volume of mail outgrew the building and the post office moved next door to its current location. In 1961, the building was purchased by attorney Scott Greene for his law office. (Courtesy of RLA.)

In 1805, the business center of Roxbury was in Shacksville, just east of Strattons Falls. The area was later called Brookdale. Shacksville had many businesses in the 1800s, including a gristmill, a sawmill, a hat factory, and a distillery. There was also a lively tavern in the area in the 1840s. The post office was in this house. The small, square structure in the forefront covered a well housing. (Courtesy of Lynda Stratton.)

This house was built by Ira Hicks in Strattons Falls, just across the road from his store. Hicks was the son of Ambrose Hicks, one of the original settlers in Meeker Hollow. In the 1930s, the house was owned by Dr. William White, a dentist in Roxbury. The front of this house is no longer visible from the road, as the road was moved and now travels along the back side of the house. (Courtesy of Lynda Stratton.)

The scenic waterfalls that give Strattons Falls its name are on the corner of Route 41 and Cold Spring Road. In this photograph, the peak of Ira Hicks's store can be seen just above the top of the falls. (Courtesy of TOR, Ronnie Ballard collection.)

The seventh of 10 children, author and naturalist John Burroughs was born in Roxbury on April 3, 1837. Burroughs had a thirst for learning and left home at age 17 to pursue teaching. He eventually settled in the Hudson Valley but returned to Roxbury in his later years. (Courtesy of RLA.)

John Burroughs spent summers in this house, Woodchuck Lodge, from 1910 through 1921. The house was built on the original Burroughs homestead property by Curtis Burroughs, John's older brother. It was owned by Henry Ford from 1922 to 1947 and then sold back to the Burroughs family. Today, tours of the home are offered during the summer months. (Courtesy of TOR, Ronnie Ballard collection.)

John Burroughs always drove Fords because his good friend Henry Ford gave him his first automobile in 1913 and kept him supplied with cars until his death. (Courtesy of the author.)

This sculpture of John Burroughs was created by Cartaino di Sciarrino Pietro and commissioned by William E. Bock. After the sculpture was completed, Bock decided that it should be enjoyed by the public and donated it to the Toledo Museum of Art. Burroughs attended the dedication ceremony in Toledo on April 12, 1918. He is seen here posing on his beloved "boyhood rock" in Roxbury as the artist works. Burroughs died in 1921 and was buried on what would have been his 84th birthday near his beloved boyhood rock. (Courtesy of TOR, Ronnie Ballard collection.)

This group of young baseball players poses for a photograph on the steps of the Roxbury School around 1900. They are partially identified as, from left to right, (first row) L. Stewart, two unidentified, ? Van Valkenburg, and ? Kilpatrick; (second row) ? Noble, ? Bouton, unidentified, and ? Aikman. (Courtesy of RLA.)

The Roxbury baseball team of the early 1900s takes a break from practice for a photograph. Town teams were made up of local farmers and tradesmen and played teams from other villages. Kirkside Park hosted many of the games. Here, Finley J. Shepard is kneeling on the far left, with Dr. Harry M. Keator next to him, and Louie Shepard is standing on the far right in a bowler hat. (Courtesy of RLA.)

The Roxbury town basketball team poses for a commemorative photograph in the late 1940s. The team, sponsored by Briggs Lumber Company, included, from left to right, (first row) Guy Numann, Carroll Hinkley, unidentified, Floyd Ploutz Jr., and Robert Munro; (second row) Virgil Slauson, unidentified, Robert Schuman, Raymond Slauson, Herbert Van Valkenburg, and Jack Lutz. (Courtesy of RLA.)

Walter Meade was a descendant of the pioneering Meade family of Batavia-Kill. He farmed in Montgomery Hollow for 30 years and, after giving up farming, devoted himself to writing, teaching, and photographing nature. He was a teacher and later became the director of the Manhattan Country School in Roxbury. He also wrote for several local magazines and newspapers. His book *In the Mountains* features his writing and many of his beautiful nature photographs. (Courtesy of Virginia Scheer.)

Irma Mae Griffin wrote several editions of the *History of the Town of Roxbury*. Born in Denver on May 22, 1903, she lived in Roxbury for all but a few years of her life. After attending Oneonta Normal School, Griffin taught for a few years before returning to Roxbury to work at the Gold Seal Assurance Society until it closed in 1929. In addition to researching and writing Roxbury's history, Griffin wrote for four local newspapers. She was the Roxbury correspondent for the *Catskill Mountain News* for more than 50 years. Local residents could expect a phone call now and then, with Griffin asking, "Any news?" If the answer was no, the conversation ended immediately so she could get on to the next call. She was honored in August 1987 at Irma Mae Griffin Day, sponsored by the Town of Roxbury. She died on October 26, 1987. (Courtesy of TOR, Ronnie Ballard collection.)

Four

FARMING IN ROXBURY

This photograph shows the framing of a large barn that was just north of the Roxbury village on Route 30. Jonas More bought the land in 1790. It was farmed by him and then by his grandson Otis Monroe Preston until 1869. The farm had a large expanse of flat fields, a rarity in the Roxbury area. (Courtesy of TOR, Ronnie Ballard collection.)

These two houses were built by Jonas More. The smaller house in the forefront, built in 1795, was the first home of Jonas and Deborah More. When the larger house was completed in 1818, the family moved into it, and the smaller house became the tenant house. It burned in 1975. (Courtesy of TOR, Ronnie Ballard collection.)

The large farmhouse was dismantled, stored, and eventually donated to the Farmers Museum in Cooperstown, New York, in 1996. It has since been reassembled and is now part of the museum's Historic Structures display. (Courtesy of TOR, Ronnie Ballard collection.)

The Jonas More farm was purchased by Irving Tyler in 1874, and the Tyler family farmed the land for 83 years. The main barn and the various other outbuildings are seen here, with Route 30 just visible at the bottom of the photograph. The Tyler family sold the farm to Earl Wright Sr. in 1957. The fine, flat fields are still in use today, growing corn and produce. The barns and houses are gone, but the area is still known as Wright's Flats. (Courtesy of TOR, Ronnie Ballard collection.)

The large fields owned by Daniel Tyler in the 1920s were ideal landing spots for barnstormer pilots. This plane, piloted by Basil Rowe of Shandaken, is seen on August 20, 1921. Rowe offered plane rides to people for $10, and many daring residents took advantage of the offer. (Courtesy of RLA.)

Abraham Gould and his family came to Roxbury around 1792. His second child, John Burr Gould, who was born in Roxbury in 1792, inherited the family farm on West Settlement Road. John's son Jason "Jay" Gould did not aspire to farming for his own career, and in 1852, John Burr Gould sold the family farm and moved to the village, where Jay began working in the family hardware business. (Courtesy of TOR, Ronnie Ballard collection.)

George Bouton owned the original Gould farm for many years, passing it on to his son Charles. Lynn and Bertha Slauson Cammer purchased the farm in 1934 and farmed there until Lynn's death in 1956. Bertha sold the farm and moved to town in 1961. (Courtesy of Daniel Underwood.)

This photograph was taken while the original Gould farm was owned by Charles Bouton by Charles's sister Lena Bouton Underwood. She was a well-known photographer in the area, documenting people, schools, and the ever-changing landscape. (Courtesy of Daniel Underwood.)

The Montgomery family came to Roxbury in 1806 with a cow and a horse. The family settled on Fredenburgh Road, in an area of Roxbury known as Montgomery Hollow. This house was built by Hiram Montgomery near the original family home. The last Montgomery descendant to live in the house was Dorcas Bartley, who named the farm Los Olmos for the large elm trees growing there. (Courtesy of Daniel Underwood.)

This view of Martin Cantwell's farm shows a very different Route 30 just south of Roxbury. The road is nothing more than a one-lane dirt track mirrored by carefully laid stone walls. The house was eventually moved across the road. The barn is gone, but remnants of its foundation are still visible. (Courtesy of TOR, Ronnie Ballard collection.)

This was the farm of Carroll Hinkley, a prominent farmer and the Roxbury town supervisor from 1938 to 1947 and 1950 to 1951. The farm was also the site of a former tannery. The next owner of the farm was James Hinkley. The Darling family currently owns and runs the dairy farm. (Courtesy of TOR, Ronnie Ballard collection.)

This west-facing view shows the farm of Richard Bouton in 1961. The farm is just south of the village on Route 30. Bouton was one of the last farmers to operate a dairy farm around the village of Roxbury. The main barn and a small tenant house are seen here. (Courtesy of RLA.)

The Meeker family came to Roxbury around 1800. Lyman and Salome Meeker and their 11 children were a pioneer family, and Meeker Hollow was named after them. After one of their children took over the Meeker Hollow farm, Lyman and Salome moved to the farm below, named Orchardside, on Orchard Street (Route 30) on the south edge of the hamlet of Roxbury. (Courtesy of TOR, Dick Bouton collection.)

Jacob Cornelius Keator was the son of Cornelius Keator, a 1797 pioneer settler in the Brookdale area, south of Roxbury near Briggs Road. A successful farmer and landowner, Keator owned several farms in the area. The men above take a break from farm work at one of Keator's barns. (Courtesy of TOR, Ronnie Ballard collection.)

Pauline Clark grew up on Sunnyside Farm on Carroll Hinkley Road. Pauline, her twin, Paul, and the rest of the Clark siblings attended Cold Spring School, district No. 12. The children walked the two-mile route to school. Pauline is posing here in front of the family barn and silo. Long after the Clark family had moved on from this farm, in the mid-1980s, the silo was destroyed by a twister. (Courtesy of Patricia Bussy.)

Orley Slauson and two of his eight children, Grant and Huldah, are seen here. Slauson bought the lower farm on New Kingston Mountain Road some time around 1920. His son Floyd was the next owner. The farm was sold to James Perkins in 1966 and later became the Manhattan Country School. (Courtesy of Cathy Cammer.)

Branching off from Lower Meeker Hollow Road, New Kingston Mountain Road heads over the mountain into the village of New Kingston. Two farms occupied this side of the mountain. This photograph shows the original road and the lower farm, owned by Luther Whipple Jr. and later by Floyd Slauson. It is now part of the Manhattan Country School, and students spend time at the farm school as part of their regular curriculum. Starting in the second grade, they spend a few days at the farm, and by eighth grade, they spend several weeks there. Nature studies and weaving are some of the activities they learn, along with doing farm chores. (Courtesy of the author.)

Birch Hinkley was the first Hinkley to move to the Roxbury area. Originally from Dutchess County, he settled in the Vega Valley. Hinkley's son Edward, who was born in 1830, is seen here. He married Sara Caroline Pulling in 1855, and they ran the family farm in Meeker Hollow with their three sons. (Courtesy of the author.)

This is the farm of Samuel and Abigail Pulling on Upper Meeker Hollow Road. The Pullings began farming in the hollow in the 1820s. Their daughter Sara Caroline Pulling married Edward Hinkley. The farm remained in the Hinkley family for many years, passing from father to son. Scott, Winfield, and Thomas Hinkley were the subsequent owners. The farmhouse was finally sold out of the Hinkley family in 1987. (Courtesy of Jeannine Hinkley.)

In 1802, the Little Delaware Turnpike was built, connecting Delhi, Bovina, Meeker Hollow, and Roxbury. This stone building on the turnpike route was originally built as a tavern in 1803 on the Ambrose Hicks farm. The tavern operated for 20 years. Hicks sold the farm to his son Ira, who later moved to Strattons Falls. (Courtesy of John Burrows.)

More Settlement was between Grand Gorge and Roxbury. John T. More built his farm in this valley in 1813. When his mother became ill, he and his youngest brother, Edward, traded homes. Edward, with his family and Moresville founders John and Betty More, moved to the stone farm house, and John T. took over the tavern in Moresville, where Routes 23 and 30 intersect in Grand Gorge. Edward built the stone house in 1829. (Courtesy of the author.)

Five

BUSINESS IN ROXBURY

A man and his young son stand in front of one of the earliest stores in Roxbury on upper Main Street. William Decker built the store, a tavern, and a dwelling in 1823. After 12 years, the store burned, and Decker moved away. The store was rebuilt and operated for many years, closing in the 1890s, when the arrival of the railroad and the location of the depot caused the business center of Roxbury to move farther south. (Courtesy of RLA.)

CAPITOL THEATRE
ROXBURY, N. Y.   PHONE 16
25c ADULT ADMISSION — Any Seat — Anytime
Children Under 12 — 10c; Students 12 and Over, 15c
GOOD WILL NIGHT every WED. & SAT., from $20 to $100 in CASH FREE

WED., SEPT. 29—GOOD WILL NITE—2 Shows: 7:15 & 9

SING WITH 'EM! LAUGH WITH 'EM!
LOVE WITH 'EM! LET YOURSELF GO!

'SING AND BE HAPPY'

SEE IT
AND SING!
Five bit tunes
by Sidney Clare
and Harry Akst

ANTHONY MARTIN · LEAH RAY
JOAN DAVIS · HELEN WESTLEY
ALLAN LANE · DIXIE DUNBAR

THURS. and FRI., SEPT. 30-OCT. 1—1 Show at 8:00 P.M.

Rudyard Kipling's
WEE WILLIE WINKIE

SHIRLEY TEMPLE
and
VICTOR McLAGLEN

with C. AUBREY SMITH · JUNE LANG
MICHAEL WHALEN · CESAR ROMERO

The Capitol Theatre (above) was built in 1924 by Maurice Fanning. The new theater seated around 400 people. The first movie to play there was *The Hunchback of Notre Dame* on August 23, 1924. The theater declined and closed in the mid-1950s, as more people owned televisions and went to the movies less often. After the theater closed, the building housed auctions, real estate offices, and, most recently, a pharmacy, which is now also closed. (Courtesy of RLA.)

This playbill for the Capitol Theatre advertises movies from 1937. Calling the theater only required two digits, and a ticket to the movies appears to have been a great bargain, although quarters and dimes were often hard to come by in the 1930s. Good Will Night featured an opportunity for patrons to win a drawing for a cash prize. (Courtesy of Marion Gile.)

FRIDAY SATURDAY
OCT 1-2
FROM THE HEART OF TEXAS TO THE BANKS OF THE
RIO GRANDE...They Blazed a Desperate Trail!

THREE YOUNG STARS CREATE AN EXCITEMENT ALL THEIR OWN!

Three
Young
Texans
TECHNICOLOR

Mitzi   Keefe   Jeffrey
GAYNOR · BRASSELLE · HUNTER

PLUS CO-FEATURE

"FIREMAN,
SAVE MY CHILD!"

SPIKE JONES
and his CITY SLICKERS
BUDDY HACKETT · HUGH O'BRIAN
ADELE JERGENS · TOM BROWN

COMING SOON
REAR WINDOW, SABRINA, DRAGNET,
THE COMMAND.

BOXHOLDER
OR
STAR ROUTE

Sec. 562, P. L. & R.
U. S. POSTAGE
1¢¢ PAID
Roxbury, N.Y.
Permit No. 2

CATO SHOW PRINT   CATO, N.Y.

CAPITOL THEATRE
Roxbury, New York   -   Phone 3671

Fri. - Sat. Last Complete Show 8:30
Sunday From 7:00 to 11:00 Continuous
Monday One Show At 8:00

SUN. MON.   SEPT 12-13

Cecil B. DeMille's
THE
GREATEST SHOW
ON EARTH   Technicolor

BETTY   CORNEL   CHARLTON
HUTTON · WILDE · HESTON

FOR THIS SHOW ONLY....
SUN.. ONE SHOW STARTS 7:30
MON...ONE SHOW STARTS 8:00

This is possibly one of the last handbills from the Capitol Theatre, as these movies were shown in 1954 and the theater closed around that time. These handbills were mailed to community members. (Courtesy of RLA.)

The Cities service station was built in 1920 on the site of the Clarmont Hall. It was owned by Henry W. Morse. In 1949, LaMoure "Stub" Stewart and his son Herbert Paul "Ducky" Stewart were partners in the business. LaMoure continued to run the business alone after his son's death in 1973. The gas station closed in 1975 and was torn down in 1976. (Courtesy of TOR, Ronnie Ballard collection.)

A Business Block, Roxbury-in-the-Catskills.

The first building on the left in this photograph is the Enderlin Hardware Store. Frank Enderlin purchased the store from Alexander Burhans in 1895. The Enderlin family operated the hardware store for 75 years. Frank ran the business until his death in 1946. At the time, he was the oldest businessman in Roxbury. His son F. Leighton Enderlin then took over, operating the business until 1965. (Courtesy of Lynda Stratton.)

This building was originally on the corner of Main and Bridge Streets. Around 1840, it was moved to its present location by Edward Burhans. It was rebuilt by Alexander Hamilton Burhans around 1850. Known as the yellow store, the business went through many owners before being bought by Raymond F. Cronk, who rented it to the Victory Chain, Inc., which operated the store until 1954. On January 1, 1956, the Roxbury Post Office moved into the building. (Courtesy of the author.)

Formerly the site of a barn owned by the Roxbury Hotel, this building was erected as a store by partners Alexander Hamilton Burhans and Dr. Jacob Newkirk. Various other storekeepers followed. It was the first location of Charles Gorsch's undertaking establishment, and the rear of the building housed Roxbury's first drugstore. The Gold Seal Assurance Society used the north side of the building from 1902 until 1930. The building also housed many law offices over the years and was eventually turned into apartments. (Courtesy of Lynda Stratton.)

Arthur F. Bouton was secretary-treasurer of the Gold Seal Assurance Society in the early 1900s. He is seen here, in the back row wearing a necktie, with his staff in his offices in the Gold Seal Building. The woman standing front and center is Irma Mae Griffin, who wrote *The History of the Town of Roxbury* in 1953 and updated it in 1975. (Courtesy of RLA.)

This large building replaced a smaller building on the corner of Route 30 and Bridge Street some time before 1840. The Corner Store was a general store with customers coming from as far away as Griffins Corners (Fleischmanns). Future multimillionaire Jay Gould clerked at the store for owner Edward I. Burhans in his early youth. Burhans represented Delaware County in the New York State Assembly in 1844, was a state senator from 1858 to 1859, and returned to the assembly in 1868. (Courtesy of TOR, Ronnie Ballard collection.)

The National Bank of Roxbury opened on May 1, 1905, in the Gold Seal Building. The bank building, seen here, was completed that summer and opened for business on August 28, 1905. Frank M. Andrus was president and Arthur Bouton was vice president. Shareholder Helen Gould Shepard bailed out the bank with private funds during the Great Depression. In recent years, the building was home to the Roxbury Arts group and named the Old Bank Gallery. (Courtesy of RLA.)

This photograph looks south on Main Street, with the Roxbury Hotel straight ahead. Route 30 veered off to the left just before the hotel. The first building on the right is Minnerly's drugstore. Walter H. Minnerly learned the druggist trade in Tarrytown, New York, when he was just 15. He moved to Roxbury at age 21 to start his own drugstore in 1895. (Courtesy of Lynda Stratton.)

Florence Groton built this store in 1898 to house her dry goods store. She operated the store until 1910, when she sold it to sisters-in-law Amy and Eva O'Kelly, who ran the store for 10 years. Walter H. Minnerly purchased the building and moved his drugstore into the larger space in 1920. (Courtesy of TOR, Ronnie Ballard collection.)

The Brower Bros. and Long Garage building was built by Edward I. Burhans in 1840 as a town hall. It was originally called Burhan's Hall. The town hall operated on the upper floor, and the lower floor was an opera house. The addition barely visible in the left rear of the building had a floor that could be raised with a rope-and-pulley system. (Courtesy of TOR, Ronnie Ballard collection.)

The Brower Bros. and Long Garage operated from 1918 to around 1945. It continued to operate as a garage for five more years and then became a paint, linoleum, and wallpaper store owned by Bruce Caswell. It burned down on January 16, 1954, on what was reportedly the coldest night of the year. Caswell constructed a new building on the site that eventually became the kindergarten building for Roxbury Central School. A school parking lot occupies the site now. (Courtesy of TOR, Ronnie Ballard collection.)

The Reed's Taproom building was home to several businesses before becoming part of Reed's Hotel. Prior businesses included a cooper shop, a millinery shop, and a candy store that served the first ice cream in town. Three separate grocery businesses followed. Burton Reed sold furniture in the building before turning it into the taproom. Alice Reed Kasmer and her husband, Steve Kasmer, took over the taproom in 1969. Reed's Taproom closed on September 30, 2008. (Courtesy of Daniel Underwood.)

The Roxbury Esso Service Center was built in 1940 by Perry L. White and his son Douglas. Elton LaRue became the manager in 1945. It was on the site of the former Roxbury Inn, which was torn down in 1940. The station evolved into an Exxon station and has since been torn down and replaced with a convenience store and gas station. (Courtesy of Daniel Underwood.)

Above, proprietors Marion and Harold "Bud" Gile stand behind the counter of their restaurant, Bud's, in 1948. Employee Irv Tyler is on the right, Jim Hammond sits at the counter, and customer Glen Whitney stands nearby. (Courtesy of the author.)

This undated photograph was likely taken in the 1970s. Breakfast or lunch at the counter at Bud's was a daily habit for many Roxbury residents. The man wearing glasses on the left is owner Bud Gile. Along with breakfast or lunch, one could buy shoes, clothing, sunglasses, and toys, which were just a few of the items Bud's offered. (Courtesy of Perry White.)

This ornate building housed a shoe store and then a jewelry store before being bought by Maurice H. Fanning in 1908. Fanning sold jewelry, stationery, and optometry services there. He moved his store to a bigger building around 1920. Following business included two barbershops, a telephone office, and a restaurant. Around 1970, the building was purchased by Harrison and Linden Morse and torn down. Eventually, the Morse brothers utilized the space to expand their insurance office. (Courtesy of TOR, Ronnie Ballard collection.)

The original Methodist church building is seen below in the 1930s, when it was a grocery store. When a new church building was planned, this old building was moved south to become a chapel and lecture hall for the Roxbury Academy. Later, it housed a meat market and then this grocery store. The building was purchased by Harrison and Linden Morse in 1969 to house their insurance business. When the Morse Insurance office relocated, this building was transformed into apartments. (Courtesy of TOR, Ronnie Ballard collection.)

As settlers cleared the forests, it became apparent that the uneven land and plentiful springs and brooks made Roxbury a natural dairy region. The Cold Spring Creamery was one of many creameries in the area, and operated from 1899 to 1936. It was south of Roxbury alongside the tracks of the Ulster & Delaware Railroad, and it was listed as Station 56. (Courtesy of Lynda Stratton.)

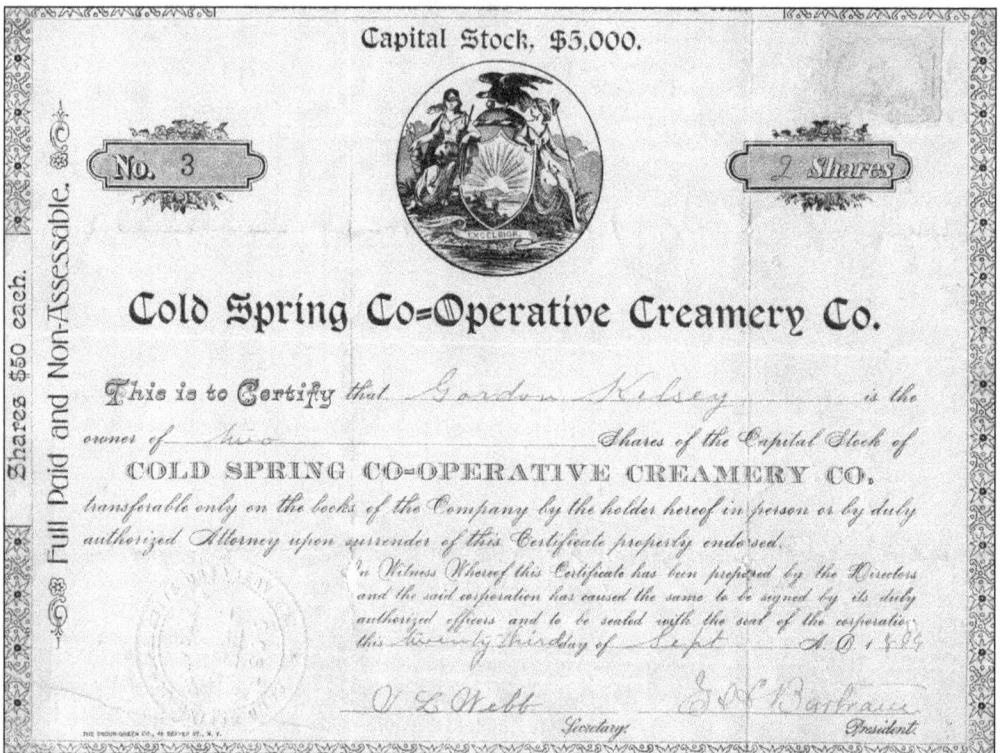

The Cold Spring Co-Operative Creamery Co. opened on April 1, 1899, at Travis Crossing, now Cold Spring Road. The first officers were George Bouton, president, and Edward Bartram, secretary. The creamery closed in 1936. The officers at that time were Scott Hinkley, president; James M. Bouton, secretary; and Bruce Mead, treasurer. (Courtesy of TOR, Ronnie Ballard collection.)

These Cold Spring Creamery employees are making cheese. The young man on the right is Herm Osche. This area of Roxbury was first called Scrubville, but when the railroad came, it was called Travis Crossing for one of its residents. When the Cold Spring Creamery was built, there was yet another name change. This name has endured, and the road where the creamery was located is still Cold Spring Road. (Courtesy of TOR, Ronnie Ballard collection.)

Samuel and Joseph Stratton came to Roxbury in 1792 and settled near the falls that bear their name. In the 1800s, Strattons Falls supported a cooper shop, a blacksmith shop, and a tavern. On December 14, 1840, a post office was established. The building seen here above the keystone bridge housed a store and the post office and was owned by Ira Hicks and Lewis Stratton, who was appointed the second postmaster in 1844. Hicks was appointed postmaster after Stratton's death in 1851. (Courtesy of TOR, Ronnie Ballard collection.)

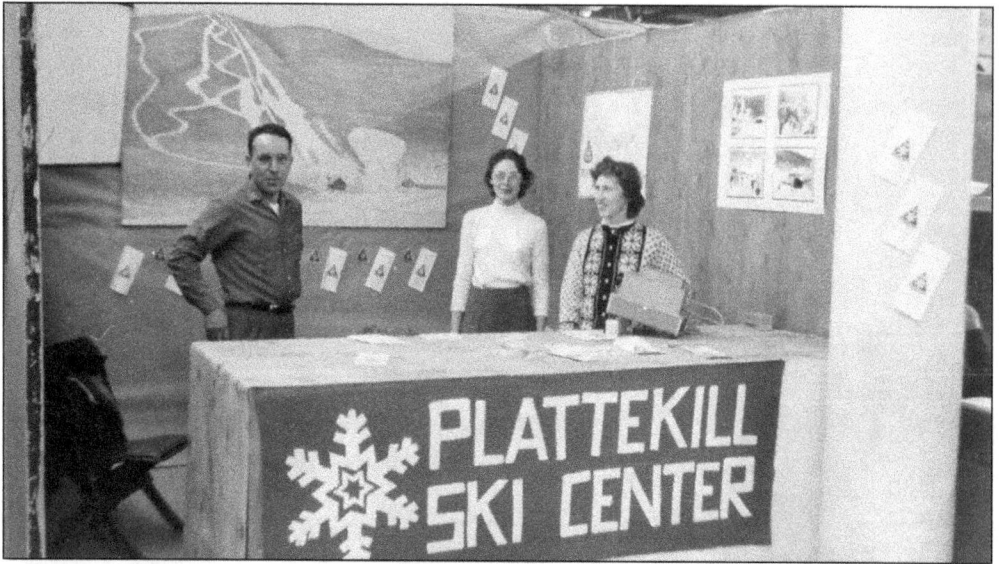

Plattekill Ski Center opened for business in 1958 in Meeker Hollow. Local builder and contractor Sanford Hinkley and his brother Gary started the ski area with a rope tow operated by an automobile motor and a small lodge. By 1961, the business had incorporated, and the officers were Sanford Hinkley, president; Gary Hinkley, vice president; and Beatrice Hinkley, secretary-treasurer. Seen here attending a promotional show in 1964 are, from left to right, Sanford Hinkley, Betty Munro, and Sanford's wife, Beatrice. (Courtesy of Beatrice Hinkley.)

Snow-covered slopes brought out the skiers in 1963. A T-bar reaching the 3,250-foot summit was completed in 1961. This view shows a full lower parking lot and a line for the T-bar. With no sitting allowed, the T-bar pushed the skier up the 3,000-foot route to the top of the mountain. The view at the top and the exciting trip back down made it all worthwhile. (Courtesy of Beatrice Hinkley.)

The original 1958 lodge was only one story. Over the years, the footprint was enlarged and two stories were added. (Courtesy of Beatrice Hinkley.)

In 1971, major improvements came to Plattekill with the installation of a triple chairlift and the addition of new trails. Here, Gary Hinkley, the president of the corporation from 1970 to 1992, oversees a new south-facing trail and the construction of the new chairlift. Skiers could finally give their legs a break while traveling up the mountain. (Courtesy of Gary Hinkley.)

The Riverside Hotel on Bridge Street was a hotel and tavern from the 1880s until around 1915, when Roxbury abolished the liquor trade by local option. A.J. Shafer purchased the building on May 5, 1915, and operated a jewelry store, an ice cream parlor, and a repair service for watches, clocks, and typewriters. In 1965, Gary Hinkley bought the building and turned it into an apartment house. The property is now occupied by a wing of the Roxbury Motel. (Courtesy of TOR, Ronnie Ballard collection.)

The Log Cabin restaurant in Hubbell Corners was operated by Bill and Flora Graham in the 1920s. The Grahams raised their own chickens, retrieving and butchering them as needed for use in the restaurant. Gasoline was available for sale as well. Route 30 traveled past the restaurant and through Hubbell Corners until the road was re-routed around 1980. (Courtesy of Daniel Underwood.)

Six

THE KIRKSIDE ESTATE

Helen Gould purchased this Greek Revival–style home on Main Street, the first part of the Kirkside Estate, in 1896. The house, built by Liberty Preston in 1865, was originally a simple, seven-room home. Gould remodeled and enlarged the house over the years, creating a grand summer home named Kirkside, which means "church side." The house is now a retirement home, Kirkside of Roxbury. The home has retained its 1865 charms, and summertime porch-sitting is still a favored activity. (Courtesy of TOR, Ronnie Ballard collection.)

Marshall Dales began building Dales' Lake in 1907, hiring H.H. Vaughn of Passaic, New Jersey, to build it. The construction of the original dam is seen here. The lake was intended as a reservoir to supply the village with water and ice and for recreation for the townspeople. Dales built a small house there called the Waldorf where he sold ice cream on weekends. (Courtesy of RLA.)

This 1911 photograph shows the rebuilding of Dales' Lake financed by Helen Gould. The lake was enlarged and the dam improved at that time. The lake was renamed Kirkside Lake. Construction of this dam was far more involved than the original Dales' Lake dam but still relied heavily on manpower and horsepower. (Courtesy of RLA.)

Dales' Lake caused concern that if the dam ever broke, it would flood Bridge and Locust Streets. For that reason, Marshall Dales was more than happy to sell the lake and some property to Helen Gould in 1908, as she could afford to rebuild the lake and make it safer. She later purchased the entire Dales farm. Gould married Finley J. Shepard in 1913, and in 1916, they began building an estate golf course near the lake. (Courtesy of TOR, Ronnie Ballard collection.)

The Lake Cottage was part of the Kirkside Estate property owned by Helen Gould Shepard. It was commissioned by the Gould family in 1911 as a guesthouse for summer visitors featuring beautiful lake views. The property remained in the Shepard family until 1972, when it was sold to a private investor. Presently, the golf course is open to the public and the Lake Cottage houses the clubhouse and pro shop. (Courtesy of RLA.)

Building the road to Kirkside Lake and golf course required many hands and strong backs. Large fieldstone retaining walls were built on this portion to carve out a hairpin turn about halfway up the mountain road. The road-building crew takes a break in this photograph, relaxing in style in some of the Adirondack-style furniture featured in Kirkside Park. (Courtesy of TOR, Ronnie Ballard collection.)

The grounds crew moves a tree to its new home in this late-1930s photograph. The truck is a 1937 GMC, and the tractor doing the hauling is equipped with tracks. Kirkside Park and golf course featured many trees, native and exotic, planted by the grounds crew. (Courtesy of Daniel Underwood.)

The 10-acre lake on the Kirkside Estate was an important source of ice for the village. Ice was cut and put in icehouses and covered in sawdust. The ice-cutting plow is seen here out on the lake. The blocks of ice were used locally to keep food fresh through the warmer months. (Courtesy of Daniel Underwood.)

The ice-cutting crew takes a break from its work. The crew hauled the ice down the road to town, although some of the ice was for the Kirkside Estate. The icehouse for the estate was in one of the barns behind Helen Gould Shepard's home. Many local men were employed throughout the Depression by the Kirkside Estate. (Courtesy of Daniel Underwood.)

This car is a Locomobile, advertised as the "Best built Car in America." The Locomobile Society of America states that these cars were owned by the who's who of upper East Coast aristocracy and mentions Jay Gould as an owner. This vehicle was owned by Finley J. Shepard, Gould's son-in-law. Shepard's driver, Tom Porter, is operating the convertible roadster, and in the back seat are Ralph Ives Sr. (left) and Finley J. Shepard. (Courtesy of TOR, Ronnie Ballard collection.)

This car suffered a predictable outcome after being hit by a train. The unfortunate end for the vehicle came on August 8, 1924, at the railroad crossing near the Kirkside Park greenhouse on the road that leads to the golf course. (Courtesy of TOR, Ronnie Ballard collection.)

The building of the Kirkside Estate was started by Helen Gould in the 1890s. Kirkside Park was part of that endeavor. The park was landscaped by Ferdinand Mangold, featuring Adirondack-style bridges, gazebos, a guesthouse, and a children's playhouse. Many local men were employed to build and maintain the estate. In recent years, the park has been restored, and it is a treasured feature of Roxbury used for baseball, softball, and soccer games. It is also a beautiful location for concerts, weddings, and parties. (Courtesy of TOR, Ronnie Ballard collection.)

Maintaining the beautiful grounds of the Kirkside Estate required a crew of men, at least 25 at times. These workers take a break from work to pose with their push mowers. The back of Helen Gould Shepard's beautiful home is seen in the background to the left. (Courtesy of Jay Gould Memorial Reformed Church.)

Helen Gould married Finley Shepard in 1913. The couple is seen here on the golf course, which remained in the family until 1972, when it was sold to a private developer. Since then, it has been leased to the Shephard Hills Golf Association and is open to the public. The new spelling of Shephard was required by the terms of the sale. (Courtesy of Daniel Underwood.)

Seven

INNS AND
BOARDINGHOUSES

This beautiful home, owned by Frank Richtmyer, was named the Park View because of its location across the street from Kirkside Park. After Richtmyer's death, his widow, Mary, operated a boardinghouse in the home. After her death, her daughter, Frances Stack, sold the home to her uncle Arthur F. Bouton. It was an apartment house for some years, during which time a fire claimed the third floor. After the third floor was removed, it became a single-family home. (Courtesy of TOR, Ronnie Ballard collection.)

The intersection of Routes 30 and 23 in Grand Gorge was the site of the More Tavern. The first frame house on this site was built in 1808 near the original More log cabin. The More family ran a hotel and tavern in this location for many years, expanding the hotel in 1836 and selling it in 1853. Several owners followed, and in 1872, the hotel was purchased by George L. Shaffer and named the Shaffer House. Ward Streeter purchased the hotel in 1932 and operated it until his

death in 1939. His son Roy ran the hotel for a few months before it burned down on March 25, 1940. The large hotel had been in business for 104 years. When it burned, it contained some of the original timbers from the first frame house in the village. Famous guests of the hotel included Thomas Edison, Henry Ford, and Harvey Firestone. (Courtesy of Lynda Stratton.)

The farm of J.M. Cronk of Grand Gorge once stood where the NBT Bank is today. This photograph shows the large farmhouse and barns on a crisp, snow-covered day. In addition to their daily farm work, the Cronk family began hosting visitors around 1900. (Courtesy of Olive Van Aken.)

The impressive, elegant additions to the Cronk farmhouse are seen here. The great demand for lodging at the farm enabled the Cronk family to enlarge their home, adding much-needed space for more guests. A puzzling assortment of people, cars, and cows mingle in this photograph, and the many outbuildings and barns needed for farming are seen as well. (Courtesy of Olive Van Aken.)

Finely dressed guests play croquet and enjoy a summer day at the Cronk farm. The popular boardinghouse stopped hosting guests in the 1950s. The stately building was eventually sold out of the Cronk family, and it burned in 1988. (Courtesy of Olive Van Aken.)

The well-manicured lawn of the William F. Proper family home is seen here in the 1930s. The shaded porch offered a pleasant spot for guests to relax. The house is located on Route 23 just west of the village square. (Courtesy of Lynda Stratton.)

In 1885, John F. Schulteis purchased a quarry from Andrew Schuman. He then built an exclusive club on the property, naming it the Ironwood Post. It featured formal gardens, fountains, patios, stables, a wine cellar, and a dance hall. Guests included visitors from New York City and well-to-do locals. Eventually, Schulteis went bankrupt. A boardinghouse and a summer camp business followed. The camp closed in 1963, and by 1973, the property was in complete disrepair. (Courtesy of the author.)

9—Welcome Rest Farm House, Roxbury, N. Y.

This farmhouse was owned by John and Fannie Bartram. Their daughter Nellie McIntosh later ran Welcome Rest Farm, a boardinghouse for summer visitors, in the home. Nellie McIntosh sold the house to Floyd Christian in 1952. (Courtesy of Lynda Stratton.)

F. Bruce and Nellie Montgomery Easton purchased this house in 1913. After enlarging and renovating it, they ran it as a summer boardinghouse named Maplehurst. After their deaths, Maplehurst was sold in 1943. The business changed hands several times. In 1961, it was purchased by Biagio and Concetta DeLuca. They ran Benny's Italian Restaurant there for 11 years. The DeLucas beautified the property, as seen in this photograph. In 1973, Gilbert and Noreen Furman bought the business. (Courtesy of the author.)

The Lea Croft, or "meadow farm," was first owned by the Squires brothers. Around 1900, Melvin and Eva Parsons owned the home and boarded summer visitors. Relocating from their Meeker Hollow farm, Henry and Margaret Blythe purchased the Lea Croft in 1923 and continued the business. The property adjoining the house included all of what is now Roosevelt Avenue. The first two homes built on Roosevelt Avenue were for the Blythe children, Cornelius Blythe and Pauline Blythe Long. After Henry Blythe's death, the land was sold and more houses were built. The building was eventually torn down for the new National Bank of Roxbury building. (Courtesy of TOR, Ronnie Ballard collection.)

ROXBURY INN. ROXBURY. N.Y.

After the Roxbury Academy closed, Dr. John Keator turned the building into the Shady Lawn Hotel. Eugene Keator, the next owner, renamed it Central House. In 1911, the building was purchased by J. Frisbee and Minnie Bouton, who named it the Roxbury Inn. In 1928, Bruce and Clementine Kilpatrick purchased it, running a hospital there in addition to the inn. In 1938, the inn was used as a temporary school until the new school was completed. The building was demolished in the spring of 1940. (Courtesy of RLA.)

The back part of Reed's Hotel was built in the mid-1800s, when a sash and blind factory and sawmill were operated there by Gordon Ganoung. The grand Victorian addition was constructed in 1905. It is the only surviving example of the six hotels that once flourished in Roxbury. (Courtesy of the author.)

Fred Dixon was the first to run a boardinghouse, under the name Dixon Manor, at what later became Reed's Hotel. In 1918, the building was purchased by Abram and Ida Reed, the first of three generations to run the hotel. The house featured a beautiful porch for guests to relax on and enjoy the fresh country air. (Courtesy of Lynda Stratton.)

William D. House rebuilt a smaller hotel to create the Roxbury Hotel in 1880. Townspeople were excited to have an up-to-date hotel in town and were willing to pay $5 a meal to support the business. Town meetings were held at the hotel, and the newspaper publishing office was there. The second floor featured a ballroom. William House died in the fall of 1881, and several innkeepers owned it after him, the final one being T. James Porter. (Courtesy of DCHS, Bob Wyer collection.)

This south-facing view of the Roxbury Hotel shows the original path of Route 30. Once faster-moving automobile traffic became the norm, there was a need to straighten out the course of the road. The hotel was a victim of progress and was torn down on Memorial Day weekend in 1965 to make room for the relocation of Route 30. (Courtesy of the author.)

Tom and Mary Porter pose with Herbert Smith (right) as they prepare to serve a dinner for the University of Michigan Alumni Association on June 3, 1949. The weekend-long event was described in a local newspaper as "business with pleasure." Attendees traveled from all over the northeast, including Canada. They were entertained with golf, swimming, boating, softball, and a special movie screening of It Happens Every Spring. (Courtesy of RLA.)

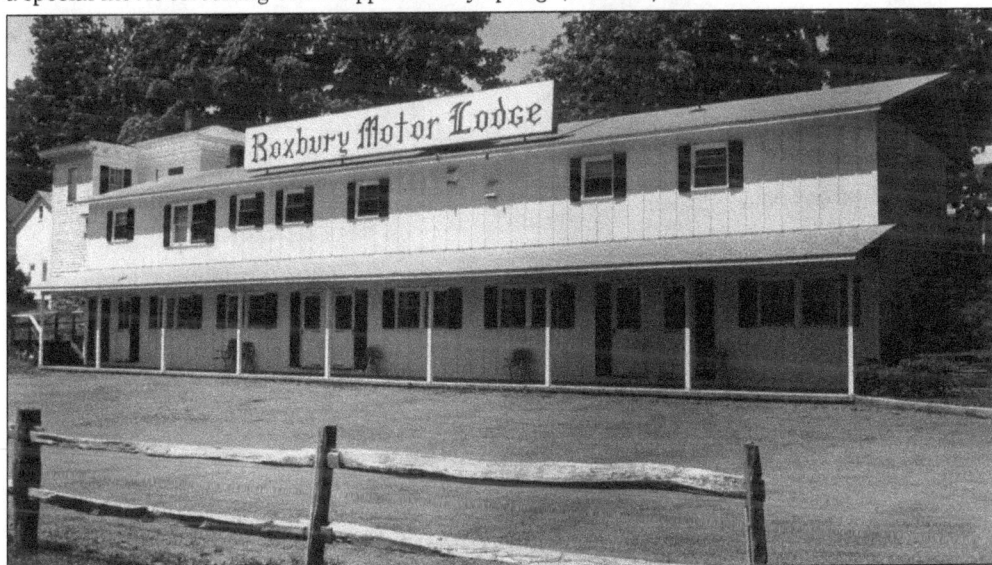

The Roxbury Motor Lodge, on the corner of Bridge and Locust Streets, was built by Gary Hinkley in 1964. It featured nine units and one efficiency apartment. It evolved into apartments, and in 2004, it was purchased by Joseph Massa and Greg Henderson. It has been completely renovated and is now The Roxbury, a "boutique resort motel" featuring uniquely decorated theme rooms. It has undergone several expansions to accommodate its growing popularity. (Courtesy of RLA.)

In 1923, the farmhouse on the right was known as Jessie's Manna Farms. It was owned by famous tenor Jules Bledsoe, who named it in the memory of his mother. Bledsoe was known for his 1929 performance of "Old Man River" in the musical *Show Boat*. After his death in 1943, the property was owned by his nephew Alvin Bledsoe Cobb. Archie McAlonen purchased the building in 1950 and ran a hotel and tavern there called McAlonen's Poplar Inn. (Courtesy of TOR, Dick Bouton collection.)

The Valley Ramblers, a popular local band, are seen at a 1986 engagement at the T-Bar, formerly McAlonen's Poplar Inn. From left to right are Leroy Slater, Bob ?, Ed Bender, Ron Berry, Gene Cronk Sr., and John Rice. The Valley Ramblers played venues from barns to schools to taverns and played tunes for round and square dancing. (Courtesy of Gene Cronk.)

Eight

SCHOOL DAYS

No one knows exactly why this stone building is called the Old Stone Jug. It was built in 1813 by David Corbin, a Quaker carpenter, and used as a schoolhouse, which John Burroughs attended in 1843. Classes ceased in 1845, and students attended West Settlement School. Later, the building was home to a Christian church. It has been a private home since the early 1900s, changing hands more than a few times. (Courtesy of TOR, Ronnie Ballard collection.)

The Grand Gorge School District No. 19 spanned from 1835 to 1929. This large group of students and teachers is standing in front of the schoolhouse built in 1889. Students who wished to continue their education past the eighth grade traveled to Roxbury. This building was used for 40 years until the district was centralized. (Courtesy of RLA.)

The Grand Gorge Central School District was established on June 4, 1929. It combined the village school and districts 10, 14, 16, and 20. This new building was constructed on the site of the former school and the lot next door, where the Reformed church had stood. The school was dedicated on October 18, 1930, and operated for 50 years, graduating more than 700 students. The building is now home to the civic center and senior apartments. (Courtesy of Preston Van Dusen.)

The More Settlement District No. 2 was located on the corner of Route 30 and Dugan Hill Road, between Roxbury and Grand Gorge. The first school building was a log building, followed by a red schoolhouse built in 1860. Later, the white building above replaced the red schoolhouse. As it was built on a rock, it was nicknamed "the schoolhouse on the rocks." The school consolidated with Roxbury School in 1930 and closed for good in 1940. (Courtesy of RLA.)

These students from Brookdale District No. 4 take part in a field day in the late 1930s. The Brookdale schoolhouse, built in 1875 at a cost of $300, is still standing on Scott Greene Road in Roxbury. Local photographer Lena Underwood took this photograph, which features her son Daniel holding the left pole of the Brookdale banner. Ronnie Ballard is holding the right pole of the China banner. (Courtesy of Daniel Underwood.)

School was first taught in Vega in a log cabin built around 1800. The school was District No. 8. A little red schoolhouse followed. This building was probably constructed around 1880. The district consolidated with Roxbury Central School in 1930, but the school remained open for grades one through six until 1953. (Courtesy of Betty Sherwood.)

A memento provided for students in 1912, this two-part, ribbon-tied booklet listed students, officers, and the teacher. Vega farmer Charles V. Cartwright was the trustee. (Courtesy of Betty Sherwood.)

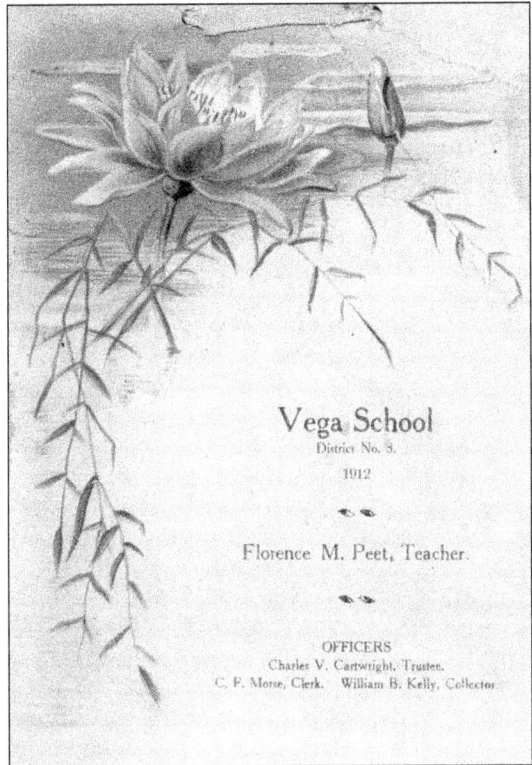

Vega School
District No. 5.
1912

Florence M. Peet, Teacher.

OFFICERS
Charles V. Cartwright, Trustee.
C. F. Morse, Clerk.   William B. Kelly, Collector.

PUPILS

Leonil B. Lead 16
      Harris S. Ballard 16
            Cornelus H. Ploutz 14
Floyd V. Sherwood 14
      Bruce L. Ford 13
            James Ploutz 13
Edward Ploutz 9
      Marvin Lawrence 12
            George Hess 11
Ward Loucks 10
      Clayton Loucks 10
            Marshall Winchell 9
Arthur Loucks 6
      Effie A. Harrington 13
            Edna George 14
Orra A. Ballard 13
      Mary Loucks 12
            Carrie Angle 11
Marian Winchell 10
      Edith Kelly 13

Many of the students listed in this 1912 booklet have familiar surnames, descended from original Batavia-Kill settlers. Students ranged in age from 6 to 16, making the teaching duties of one lone teacher very challenging. (Courtesy of Betty Sherwood.)

The Teachers Institute was a conference held each autumn. Teachers from Delaware County attended the weeklong event for training and socializing. Roxbury hosted the event several times. Lodging for the teachers was available at the Roxbury Academy and in local homes. This group photograph was taken at the Methodist church in Roxbury, where some of the meetings were held. (Courtesy of RLA.)

The Roxbury Academy was built in 1856 by John William McLaury, who thought a boarding school would be successful in Roxbury. The site was previously home to a schoolhouse built by Edward I. Burhans. Students from all over the state attended the new academy as well as local students who could afford the tuition. Girls and boys were housed in separate sides of the building. The academy closed in 1868. (Courtesy of Daniel Underwood.)

ROXBURY ACADEMY.

The Winter Term of This Institution will commence WEDNESDAY, December 1st, and continue Fourteen Weeks.

J. W. McLAURY, Principal, *Mathematics and Natural Sciences.*
N. B. FLINT, *Assistant Teacher in Mathematics.*
Rev. W. E. TURNER, A. M., *Ancient Languages and Moral Science.*
Miss E. M. EATON, *Vocal and Instrumental Music.*
Miss MARY McLAURY, Preceptress, *Ornamental Branches.*
Mrs. C. PARRISH, Matron, *Primary Department.*

EXPENSES
FOR TERM OF FOURTEEN WEEKS.

Tuition, in Common English Branches.....................$3 75	Vocalization.....................$10 00
Higher English Branches.....................5 00	Harmony and Thorough Bass.....................10 00
Classic Languages.....................6 00	Painting in Oil.....................8 00
French or German, each.....................5 00	Figures in Pastello.....................6 00
Drawing and Painting in Water Colors, each.....................3 50	Monochromatics and Ornamental Leather Work, each.....................3 00
Music on Piano, and use of Instrument.....................10 00	Wax Fruit and Flowers.....................6 00
Melodeon and Organ Music, each.....................10 00	Incidentals.....................25
Violin and Violincello, each.....................8 00	

The price of Board, including Washing, is $2 per Week. Each Student is charged $1 per Term for Wood. Students furnish their own Brooms, Towels, Toilet Soap, Lights, and Matches.

The whole expense for Board, Washing, and Incidentals, per Term of Fourteen Weeks, is $33, payable in advance.

Our references are our Pupils, whose names are in the Catalogues.

For further particulars, and Catalogues, address the undersigned, at Roxbury, Delaware County, N. Y.

J. W. McLAURY.

October 28th, 1858.

Visitor Print, Franklin, N. Y.

This list of expenses from 1858 detailed the costs for a student who wished to board at the academy. Classes in the arts cost extra, but a wide variety of classes were available. In the 1858–1859 school year, there were 113 male students. As they were less likely to receive a good education, only 60 females attended the academy that year. (Courtesy of TOR, Ronnie Ballard collection.)

The Beechwood Seminary, seen here, was started in 1844 as a result of conflicts between the "up-renters" and the "down-renters" in West Settlement during the anti-rent war. John B. Gould and Philetus Corbin were up-renters, and they built the new school for their children to attend. It was considered unsafe to let the children of the conflicting parties associate. When the anti-rent war conflict was settled in 1850, the school was abandoned, and a new West Settlement school was built. (Courtesy of RLA.)

The residents of Roxbury were very happy in 1895, when the two-story school was rebuilt and became a graded school. Previously, children were moved from the lower floor of the school to the upper floor when they were judged ready. This group of students assembled for a school photograph in the late 1890s. (Courtesy of RLA.)

This new school building featured running water and bathrooms. A tower was added for the school bell and the town clock, a gift from Frank J. Gould. The clock was installed on September 16, 1895. In 1896, a proposition passed to establish a union free school that included a high school department. It was called the Roxbury Union Free School. In 1904, the name was changed to Roxbury High School. (Courtesy of Lynda Stratton.)

34—Roxbury High School, Roxbury, N. Y.

This new, more spacious Roxbury High School was built in 1913. The building cost just over $13,000 to complete. Over its 25 years in service, 292 children graduated from the school. When Roxbury needed to expand the school once again, the clock was relocated next door to the Methodist church. (Courtesy of the author.)

In 1938, the community voted to construct a new school with the acceptance of a Public Works Administration grant totaling $133,650. The total cost for the new building was $297,000. The cornerstone was laid on May 19, 1939, and students began classes in the new building on September 25, 1939. (Courtesy of RLA.)

Program
Corner Stone Ceremonies
Roxbury Central School
May 19, 1939

Wm J. Krum, Jr.

Presentation of Master of Ceremonies..... Martin G. Cantwell
Pres. Board of Education

Scripture Reading, Proverbs 4:1-13 .... Rev. Harry Williams

Invocation .... Rev. H. S. Van Woert

First Verse of America .... Student Body

REMARKS

Stewart H. Smith, former Principal of the Roxbury Central School

Hon. Charles C. Flaesch, Unadilla, New York

Miss Zena R. Travis, District Superintendent of Schools

Hon. Arthur F. Bouton, Roxbury, New York

Harold O. Fullerton, Architect

ADDRESSES

DON L. ESSEX, Buildings and Grounds Division, State Education Department

COLONEL M. E. GILMORE, Regional Director of the Federal Emergency Administration of Public Works

Depositing of box in the Cornerstone—President of the Board of Education, Martin G. Cantwell and Col. M. E. Gilmore

Alma Mater .... Student Body

The cornerstone ceremonies featured remarks by Roxbury graduate Zena R. Travis, who was born in Meeker Hollow on November 3, 1890. She graduated from Roxbury School in 1909 and continued her education at the Oneonta Normal School. She taught in California and in Delaware County before becoming the district superintendent of schools in 1921. She was the youngest district superintendent ever when she was hired and the oldest district superintendent when she retired 37 years later. Travis died in her family home in Meeker Hollow on June 23, 1967. (Courtesy of RLA.)

The completed Tudor-style Roxbury Central School is seen here. The central school became crowded within 20 years, and in 1958, a building was purchased across Route 30 for the kindergarten class. By 1966, two more buildings were added to the campus. In 1997, a permanent addition was built to the south end of the school. (Courtesy of RLA.)

Nine

HOUSES OF WORSHIP

The Vega Methodist Church was established shortly after 1800. This building was erected in 1844. Sitting on the front step in this photograph are, from left to right, Carrie Finch, Ora Sherwood, and Neva Streeter. In 1930, after the building was vacant for many years, the Town of Roxbury purchased the it, and it is now the Vega Hall, which has hosted community events ever since. Today, a quilting group meets in the hall on Tuesdays. (Courtesy of Betty Sherwood.)

An impressive bell tower adorned the Grand Gorge United Methodist Church. The decision to build the church was made in 1852, after the congregation had been sharing space with another church group for several years. A parsonage was constructed in 1910. Unfortunately, this beautiful church building was destroyed by a fire on July 13, 1983. The congregation carried on, and a new church building was completed and dedicated in October 1984. (Courtesy of the author.)

The first Methodist society formed in Roxbury around 1800. This building was constructed in 1858 to replace an earlier building, which was moved south on Main Street. The cost of the new church building was $4,201.31. Today, the thrice-moved town clock is maintained in the tower, and it still keeps time for the village. The installation and electrification of the clock were made possible through a gift from Finley J. Shepard. (Courtesy of TOR, Ronnie Ballard collection.)

The East Branch Baptist Church was organized on April 25, 1878. After meeting in the town hall for three years, a new church building was completed in 1881. Services were held until May 1912, and in 1916, a final service was held. In 1924, the church was sold to two local businessmen, who then sold it to the Dutch Reformed Society. The building was eventually sold to M.H. Fanning for salvage, and the Dutch Reformed parsonage was built on the lot. (Courtesy of Jay Gould Memorial Reformed Church.)

This view of the Old School Baptist Church faces south. The steps used for carriages can be seen in front of the building, and one of the two outhouses sits just behind the building. The church building is still maintained. The oldest church in Roxbury, it still hosts a once-yearly service and the occasional wedding. (Courtesy of Daniel Underwood.)

The second Old School Baptist Church of Roxbury was formed on May 1, 1816. After meeting in a schoolhouse for 17 years, construction on the new building began in 1832. The first services in the building, near Strattons Falls in Roxbury, were held in April 1833. In the accompanying cemetery, many of Roxbury's pioneers are buried, as well as some Revolutionary War soldiers. (Courtesy of Lynda Stratton.)

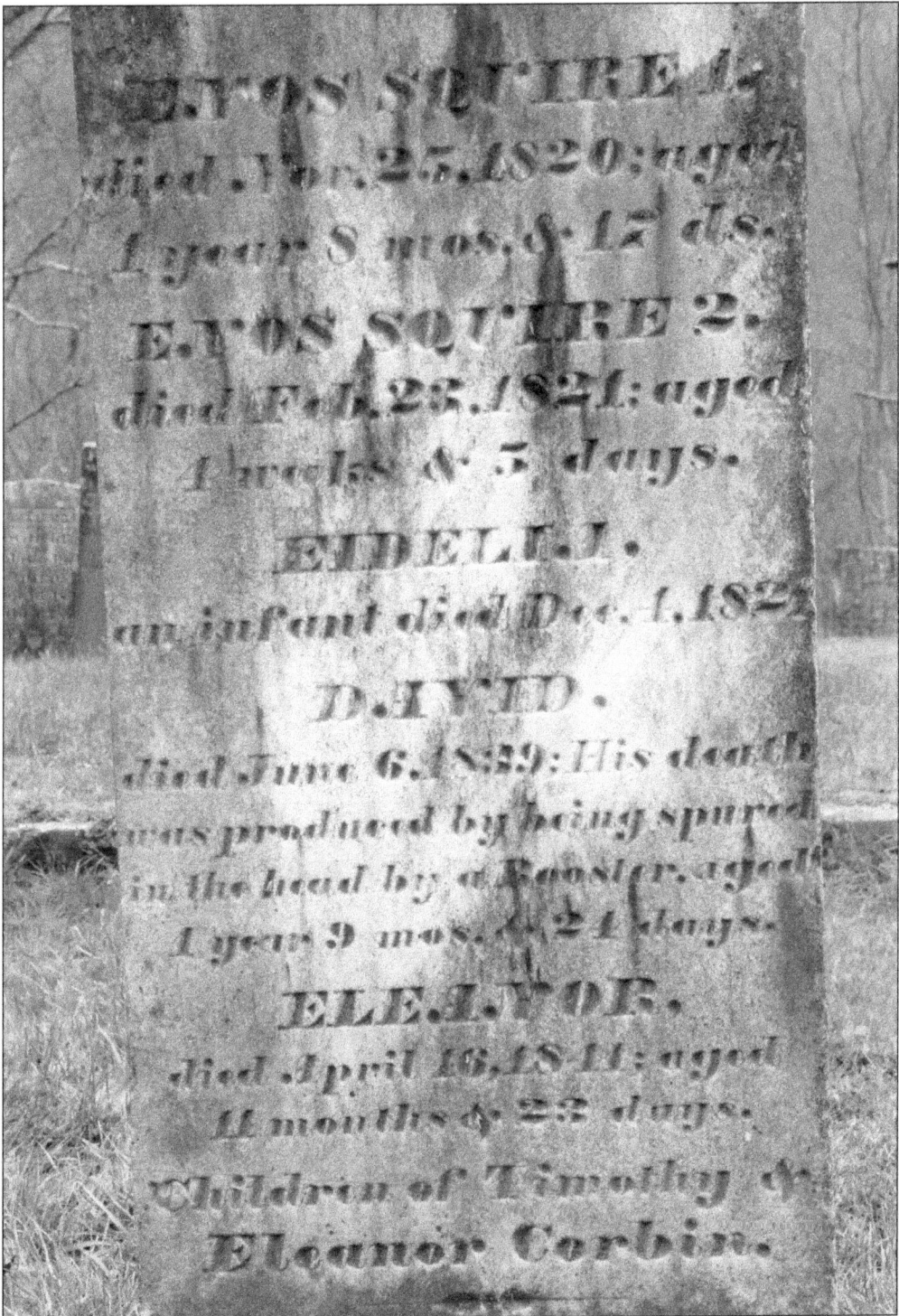

This headstone tells a sad tale of the hard times endured by Timothy and Eleanor Corbin. Five of their children are listed on the headstone; each of them died before the age of two. Their son David is listed as having died after being spurred in the head by a rooster. (Courtesy of the author.)

The Dutch Reformed Church in Roxbury began in 1802. In the following years, two church buildings were destroyed by wind and one was destroyed by fire. In the 1890s, Jay Gould promised aid for a stone church but died before any agreement had been made. The children of Jay Gould came through, providing funds and sparing no expense on the building, constructed in memory of their parents. The impressive stone structure was designed by H.J. Hardenburgh of New York City. (Courtesy of the author.)

The grand, south-facing main entrance of the church is seen here. It is constructed of St. Lawrence marble and is cruciform in shape. The carriage house is behind the church, and the rustic-style sign and entrance for Kirkside Park are visible beyond the carriage house. (Courtesy of RLA.)

Tiffany windows grace the apse and the nave of the church. The three windows in the apse depict the resurrection and show Mary, the Savior, and the Angel. Seen here, the single window in the nave represents faith, hope, and charity. The windows in the east and west wings of the church were designed by Maitland Armstrong. The east-facing window depicts Christ blessing little children, and the west-facing window shows a choir of angels. (Courtesy of TOR, Ronnie Ballard collection.)

The ground-breaking for the Jay Gould Memorial Reformed Church took place in June 1893. The cornerstone of the church was laid by George Jay Gould with a custom-made silver trowel on September 2, 1893. This large, finely dressed crowd gathered to witness the occasion. The

dedication of the completed building took place on October 13, 1894. (Courtesy of Jay Gould Memorial Reformed Church.)

Visit us at
arcadiapublishing.com

....